GREAT AMERICAN HORSES

AN IMAGINATION LIBRARY SERIES

MINIATURE HORSES

by Victor Gentle and Janet Perry

Gareth Stevens Publishing
A WORLD ALMANAC EDUCATION GROUP COMPANY

RS SD MT BM

Thanks to John and Summer Sayles; all their help and humor inspired a playful understanding of
Miniature Horses and the people who love them.
—Victor Gentle and Janet Perry

Please visit our web site at: www.garethstevens.com
For a free color catalog describing Gareth Stevens' list of high-quality books and
multimedia programs, call 1-800-542-2595 (USA) or 1-800-461-9120 (Canada).
Gareth Stevens Publishing's Fax: (414) 332-3567.

Library of Congress Cataloging-in-Publication Data

Gentle, Victor.
    Miniature horses / by Victor Gentle and Janet Perry.
        p. cm. — (Great American horses: an imagination library series)
    Includes bibliographical references (p. 23) and index.
    ISBN 0-8368-2937-9 (lib. bdg.)
    1. Miniature horses—United States—Juvenile literature. [1. Miniature horses. 2. Horses.]
    I. Perry, Janet, 1960- II. Title.
    SF293.M56G46   2001
    636.1'09—dc21   2001020850

First published in 2001 by
Gareth Stevens Publishing
A World Almanac Education Group Company
330 West Olive Street, Suite 100
Milwaukee, WI 53212 USA

Text: Victor Gentle and Janet Perry
Page layout: Victor Gentle, Janet Perry, and Scott M. Krall
Cover design: Renee M. Bach
Series editor: Katherine J. Meitner
Picture researcher: Diane Laska-Swanke

Photo credits: Cover, pp. 5 (both), 7, 9, 11, 13, 17, 19, 21, 22 © Bob Langrish; p. 15 (both) Courtesy
of John and Summer Sayles, Vintage Farms, Oregon

Printed in the United States of America

1 2 3 4 5 6 7 8 9 05 04 03 02 01

Front cover: These Miniature Horses are knee-deep in
food. They are great pets because they are small and
strong and can be fed on one backyard full of grass.

19.93

TABLE OF CONTENTS

Small Beginnings 4

Modern American Minis 6

Minis Are Horses 8

Not Falabella Horses 10

Just Right! 12

Little Big Winners 14

Horse Sense & Horse Play 16

What Makes Minis Fun? 18

A Lot of Little Horse 20

Diagram and Scale of a Horse 22

Where to Write or Call 22

More to Read and View 23

Web Sites 23

Glossary and Index 24

Words that appear in the glossary are printed in **boldface** type the first time they occur in the text.

SMALL BEGINNINGS

It took millions of years for horses to be the tall animals they are today. It only took about 100 years for Americans to produce horses that were almost as small as the horses' ancient ancestor, *Eohippus*.

How did they do this? They started by **breeding** Shetland Ponies to the small horses that used to work in coal mines. Their babies were then bred to each other to make even smaller horses.

A **breed registry** said in 1978 that any horse that was 34 inches (86 centimeters) tall or less could officially be a Miniature Horse. In 1987, the registry made a new rule. From then on, said the rule, a horse could be a registered Miniature only if both parents were also registered Miniatures.

Main: While this Mini and its ancestor, *Eohippus*, are about the same size, they are very different animals. Inset: A model skeleton of *Eohippus*.

MODERN AMERICAN MINIS

If Miniature Horses are nearly as small as *Eohippus* was, does that mean they are more like *Eohippus* than a big horse? No!

Eohippus had four little hooves on its front feet and three hooves on its back feet. It could hop better than it could run. Its short head had eyes in the front instead of on the sides, and its fur had both spots and stripes.

Like big horses, Minis have one hoof on each foot and legs that are built to run fast. They have a long head with eyes on the sides and a coat of hair that is never both spotted and striped. Miniature Horses are less like *Eohippus* and more like big wagon-pulling horses, such as Clydesdales.

A matched team of gold-colored Minis pull a wagon as finely as any big horse team.

MINIS ARE HORSES

Some people think that Miniature Horses are actually ponies because of their size. Not so! Their conformation, which is the way they are put together, is more important than their size.

Ponies are 14 hands high (hh), or less. Minis are 8 hh, or less (see page 22). Miniature Horses partly come from Shetland Ponies, but Minis are not as rounded and muscular as most ponies are. They are more like horses — slender and elegant.

Sometimes a Mini **stallion** and **mare** will have a **foal** together that is called a dwarf. Its legs, neck, and face are extra short. It cannot have any foals. It is not built like a Miniature Horse, even though it is very small.

These woolly Minis seem to be running for fun in new snow. Minis' hair grows thick for warmth in cold, just like the hair on horses and ponies.

NOT FALABELLA HORSES

Some people say that American Minis are the same as other miniature horses from other parts of the world, such as Falabella Horses. They are not.

The Falabella family found little wild horses on their land in Argentina. It was said that these horses were survivors of the **Ice Age**. There was very little to eat on the ice-covered Earth. Being smaller and needing less to eat was an advantage. As the horses mated, their smaller foals survived. So the horses got smaller with each generation.

American Minis are not descended from Falabellas. They have been bred from other breeds of horses and ponies to be the way they are.

Falabellas have the same uses as Minis and are well kept by their owners. Still, their foals will never grow to be large horses. Why do you think that is?

JUST RIGHT!

Only birds, cats, little dogs, and very small children can ride Minis. So why would you want a horse that you cannot ride? Because Minis make great pets!

Minis are perfectly sized for horse lovers who cannot control a big horse. Grown people do not ride them, but Minis do much of what big horses do.

Minis can jump in show rings. Whether alone or in teams, they pull carts, wagons, or buggies for pleasure **driving** or for obstacle course competitions. For fun, they march in parades and take part in costume contests. Many people who are too sick or too old to have their own pets love Minis — so Mini visits can be a big hit.

Elizabeth Brewer may be too small to control a full-sized horse, but this Miniature Horse is just the right size for her to handle.

LITTLE BIG WINNERS

At Vintage Farms in Oregon, Summer and John Sayles train their Minis to win big. Summer's pals are Checkers and Top Gun, or "Gunner." Checkers was the first Mini she trained. "He taught me what to do," she says, "and I applied it to Gunner."

Checkers and Gunner did a great job! Checkers was National Champion in the obstacle course. Both horses have top honors in six events (**halter**, showmanship, hunter, jumper, driving, and obstacle course). At many shows, the two Minis compete against each other, trading off first and second place.

Like any good trainer, Summer learns "which talent they are going to be really good at." She studied well!

Main: Summer with Checkers and Gunner. Inset: John and Rio share the best award of all — a cuddle.

HORSE SENSE & HORSE PLAY

John Sayles also enjoys competing in driving and halter shows with his Mini, Scribbles. They won a National Championship in the halter class, where they are judged on their looks.

To learn confidence, the Sayleses train each Mini to get around all kinds of obstacles at different speeds, again and again. Anything can happen at a show!

John and Summer's grandma showed them why confidence is important. They asked her to hold on to Checkers at a show, but he dragged her out of the barn! She was not hurt, but he knew she was unsure. Like any horse with a new rider, Checkers tested the Sayles' grandma.

These two Minis are sniffing one another to build trust. Trainers know that horses try to please anyone who understands them.

WHAT MAKES MINIS FUN?

John Sayles says that he likes to team up with Minis "because it is the one competition that I can do by myself." Summer likes taking more than one horse to each show and competing in many events. Minis are fun to show in most of the same ways that big horses are shown.

Minis are cheaper to own and train than large horses. A Mini's food is half the cost of a large horse's food. Minis also don't take up a lot of space. Half a horse stall and a backyard lot are plenty. **Tack** for Minis is cheaper, too. It is about one quarter of the cost of tack for a large horse. After all, saddles are expensive — but with Minis, you do not need one!

This young man drives a lot of horse power in a small package. Smaller tack and less food mean an owner can afford to buy some nice wheels like this!

A LOT OF LITTLE HORSE

There are plenty of reasons why Minis make great pets. Minis are every terrific thing that big horses are, except in a kid-sized package. They can do more tricks than a dog, and they are strong enough to pull a cart with you and a friend in it. They also like to please a good trainer, so they learn pretty quickly.

Whether they are pulling wagons, jumping over fences, or getting hugs, Minis are fun pals!

A mare and foal share a horse hug. The day a foal is born, its mother licks, sniffs, and nuzzles it so that they get to know each other.

DIAGRAM AND SCALE OF A HORSE

Here's how to measure a horse with a show of hands.
A longer head and slender legs mark this Mini stallion
as an American — it looks more like a horse than a pony.

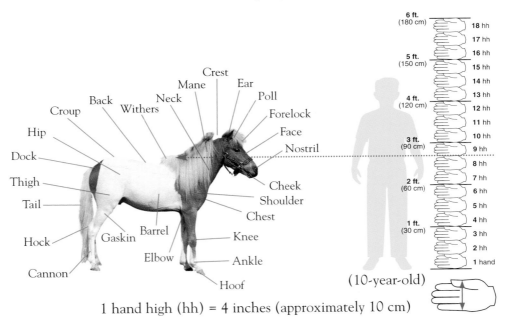

1 hand high (hh) = 4 inches (approximately 10 cm)

(10-year-old)

WHERE TO WRITE OR CALL FOR MORE INFORMATION

American Miniature Horse Association
5601 South Interstate 35W
Alvarado, TX 76009
Phone: (817) 783-5600

The American Miniature Horse Registry
81-B East Greenwood
Morton, IL 61550
Phone: (309) 263-4044

MORE TO READ AND VIEW

Books (Fiction):   *Classic Horse and Pony Stories.* (Edited by Diana Pullein-Thompson) (Dorling Kindersley)

Books (Nonfiction):   *The Complete Guides to Horses and Ponies* (series). Jackie Budd (Gareth Stevens)
Great American Horses (series). Victor Gentle and Janet Perry (Gareth Stevens)
They Dreamed of Horses: Careers for Horse Lovers. Kay Frydenborg (Walker & Co.)

Magazines: *Horse Illustrated* and its new magazine for young readers, *Young Rider Miniature Horse World*

Videos (Nonfiction):   *Eyewitness: Horse.* (BBC Lionheart/DK Vision)
Noble Horse. (National Geographic)
Ultimate Guide to Horses. (Discovery Channel)

WEB SITES

American Miniature Horse Association:
www.amha.com/amha

For more information on Miniature Horses:
www.smallhorse.com/WhatsAMini/
WhatsAMini2.html

For general horse information:
www.henry.k12.ga.us/pges/kid-pages/
horse-mania/index.htm
horsefun.com/facts/factfldr/facts.html
www.VintageFarms.net

Some web sites stay current longer than others. To find additional web sites, use a reliable search engine, such as Yahooligans or KidsClick! (http://sunsite.berkeley.edu/KidsClick!/), with one or more of the following key words to help you locate information about horses: *Eohippus, Falabellas, foals, Miniature Horses,* and *ponies.*

GLOSSARY

You can find these words on the pages listed. Reading a word in a sentence helps you understand it even better.

breed (n) — horses that share the same features as a result of the careful selection of stallions and mares to mate 4, 10

breed (past tense **bred**) (v) — to choose a stallion and a mare with certain features to make foals with similar features 4, 10

driving — making a horse in a harness pull a carriage or other vehicle 12, 14, 16, 18

foal (FOHL) — a horse under one year old 8, 10, 20

halter (HALL-ter) — leather, rope, or nylon straps fitted to a horse's head. It has no reins or mouth pieces attached to it 14, 16

Ice Age — a period that happened 10,000 to 15,000 years ago when a change in the climate of the Earth caused ice and snow to cover much of the globe 10

mare — an adult female horse 8, 20

registry (REJ-iss-tree) — a record of a horse's or a breed's ancestry 4, 22

stallion — an adult male horse 8, 22

tack — equipment fitted to and made for use on horses to lead, ride, drive, or otherwise control them for human use. Bridles, saddles, bits, stirrups, and halters are all pieces of tack 18

INDEX

Argentina 10

Brewer, Elizabeth 12

Checkers 14, 16
Clydesdales 6
conformation 8
costume contests 12

dwarf 8

Eohippus 4, 6

Falabella Horses 10

Gunner 14

Miniature Horses:
American Minis 10;
competitions 12, 14, 16;
costs of 18; features of 6;
food for 2, 10, 18;
height of 8; as pets 2, 12,
20; space needed for 18;

training of 14, 16, 20;
visits of 12

National Championships
14, 16

parades 12

Sayles, Summer and John
14, 16, 18
Scribbles 16
Shetland Ponies 4, 8